Tales from Gurbani

THE ELEPHANT KING

Written by:
Bhai Kulbir Singh Ji

Illustrated by:
Karn Parkrada

"In loving memory of Bhai Kulbir Singh Ji;
whose writings and life inspired so many countless lives."

Published in association with
Bear With Us Productions

ISBN:

Cover by Richie Evans
Design by Tommaso Pigliapochi
Illustrated by Karn Parkrada

www.justbearwithus.com

Tales from Gurbani

THE ELEPHANT KING

Written by:

Bhai Kulbir Singh Ji

Gajj means elephant.
This Gajj was Gajj-Raaj, i.e. king of elephants,
i.e. a mighty elephant who was the king of his herd.

In his previous life, this Gajj was a very pious king named **Inderduman**. He was very much inclined towards spirituality and thus gave up his kingdom and went to forests to observe austerities to please the Lord. But he had **terrible karma** from his previous lives that sprouted while he was in the forest.

One day he was sitting in meditation when the famous sage **Augustya** arrived at his ashram.

Since Inderduman was engrossed in meditation, **he did not get up** and **offer salutations** to the **arrived Sage Augustya.**

Augustya had a lot of spiritual power gained after observing penances for countless years, but he was not humble. Sage Augustya became very angry and cursed Inderduman for being dumb and not knowing how to serve and respect visitors to his house.

He cursed him as being proud and dumb like an elephant.

Inderduman accepted the curse and thus **became an elephant** in **his next life.**

After obtaining the body of an elephant,
he developed the habits and nature of an elephant.
He grew up to be a **strong elephant**
and became the **leader of his herd.**

He resided in the forests around mountain Triputi. There was a **very vast** and **beautiful lake in this forest.**

One day with his herd, he went towards the lake,
destroying vegetation and plants.
Seeing this elephant's herd coming to the lake,
all animals fled in fear.
This elephant was **very egoistic**
and thought of himself as being all-powerful.

The herd arrived at the lake and continued
with its unruly behaviour, destroying vegetation around it.
They entered the lake and **spoiled the serene
atmosphere of the lake.**

In this lake, there lived a
ColosSal OctopuS
who got **upset** at the behaviour of the elephants.

This octopus was King Huhu of Gandharv Lok, who had been arch-rival of this elephant in some previous birth.

He had received the body of an octopus because of some **bad karma** from his previous life.

The Octopus moved forward and grabbed the leg of the king of the herd.
The **elephant** and the **octopus**
were both **mighty** and **proud.**
They both had a tough fight that continued for a long time.

The **octopus**, being the creature of water, had the edge over the **elephant.**

At first other elephants tried to help him but could be of no help as they were scared of getting stuck in a similar situation.

They hesitated to go into the lake.
They stuck around for some time,
but the elephant was left **alone.**

His pride **was shattered.**
He was **losing the battle**
to this **octopus.**

Due to some **good Karma** of previous life, the elephant that by now had lost his pride and come to his senses remembered his **previous life.**

He thought to himself, that **everyone had left him** and even if they were around, they would not have been able to help him. At this time the only power who can help him is the **Lord himself.**

He remembered the **mantras** from **previous life** and called out to the **Lord** from the **bottom** of his **heart.**

It's written in Gurbani that as soon as he called to the Lord with true heart, Vaheguru immediately released the elephant from his trouble. The elephant had known Vaheguru only as Chatubhuji form. So through this form, **Vaheguru destroyed the Octopus and released the elephant.**

The octopus was killed and the elephant was released.

The octopus returned back
to his world, Gandharva Loka,
and got his position of **King Huhu.**

Due to the
grace of the Lord,
the elephant was
cleared of all his karma
and **released from
the body.**

Many pankitis in Gurbani allude to this great incident in the spiritual world and here are some examples:

Jab Hee Sharan Gahee Kirpanidh, Gajj Garah Tey Chhoota ॥
As soon as the elephant sought the protection of ocean of Mercy and Grace (Vaheguru), he was released from the clutches of the octopus.

Gajj Ko Traas Mitiyao Jih Simrat, Tum Kaahe Bisraavo ‖
Why do you forget Him, by remembering whom the fear of the elephant was removed.

Kar Dharey Chakkar, Baikunth Tey Aaye,
Gajj Hastee Ke Praan Udhareealay ‖
Vaheguru came from His abode with the
Sudarshana Chakkar in His hand,
and saved the elephant.

Some Gursikhs may have questions as to why Chaturbhuji form came to the Gajj's aid. The answer to this question is "Jaisi Mansha Taisi Dasha ||". Vaheguru gives Darshan in that form that one is seeking or one believes in. The highest Darshan of Vaheguru is His Darshan in real form i.e. Nirgun form. What Gajj or many of the older Bhagats envisioned was the Guru-Joti acting through whatever they believed was Vaheguru's form. Gursikhs who japp the Maha-Mantra, the true Mantra given by Siri Guru Nanak Dev Jee, get the highest Darshan of Vaheguru: His original form, the Nirgun form.

Printed in Great Britain
by Amazon

44326645R00018